The Two Yvonnes

PRINCETON SERIES OF CONTEMPORARY POETS

Paul Muldoon, *series editor*

For other titles in the Princeton Series of Contemporary Poets see page 60

JESSICA GREENBAUM

The Two Yvonnes

POEMS

PRINCETON UNIVERSITY PRESS
Princeton & Oxford

Copyright © 2012 by Jessica Greenbaum

Requests for permission to reproduce material from this work should be
sent to Permissions, Princeton University Press
Published by Princeton University Press, 41 William Street, Princeton,
New Jersey 08540
In the United Kingdom: Princeton University Press, 6 Oxford Street,
Woodstock, Oxfordshire OX20 1TW

press.princeton.edu

Library of Congress Cataloging-in-Publication Data
Greenbaum, Jessica.
The two Yvonnes / Jessica Greenbaum.
p. cm. — (Princeton series of contemporary poets)
ISBN 978-0-691-15662-0 (cloth : acid-free paper) —
ISBN 978-0-691-15663-7 (pbk. : acid-free paper)
I. Title.
PS3607.R446T96 2012
811'.6—dc23   2012020320

British Library Cataloging-in-Publication Data is available

This book has been composed in Garamond Premier Pro

Printed on acid-free paper. ∞

Printed in the United States of America

10   9   8   7   6   5   4   3   2   1

Cover: *Ambling Between,* by Miriam Ancis

Bella,

Becki

each,

and together

CONTENTS

ACKNOWLEDGMENTS

With gratitude to the publications in which these poems have appeared or are forthcoming:

Alaska Quarterly Review	"Firefly"
Bellevue Literary Review	"Perfume's Journey"; "The Use of Metaphor"
CCAR Journal	" 'This' and 'That' "
Cerise Press	"A Line from Jimi Hendrix Comes to Mind"; "What We Read Then"
Cincinnati Review	"Early April"
Hampden-Sydney Poetry Rev	"My Hands in Winter"; "The Gold Standard"
Harvard Review	"The First, Youngest Men"
Michigan Quarterly Review	"Promised Town"
Naugatuck River Review	"Marriage Made in Brooklyn"
The New Yorker	"Next Door"; "No Ideas but in Things"; "The Two Yvonnes"; "The Voice of Peace"
nextbook	"Cosmic Page"
Orion	"Gardens, Passover"; "One Block from the Navy Yard"
Ploughshares	"Stowaway's Ascent"
Poetry	"A Poem for S."
	"For You Today"
	"Houston in the Early Eighties"
Poetry London	"Gratitude's Anniversary"

Salamander	"Baldo's"; "Beauty's Rearrangements"; "Little White Truck"; "One Key"; "Packing Slip"; "Sonnets for the Autobiographical Urban Dweller"; "Streaming Nancy"; "Without Measure"
Talking Writing	"Before"
Verse Wisconsin	"The Moment We Can't Stay"
Women's Review of Books	"Anthology"

"The First, Youngest Men" and "Little White Truck" also appeared on *Poetry Daily*
"A Line from Jimi Hendrix Comes to Mind" also appeared on *Verse Daily*
"No Ideas but in Things" was reprinted in *Best Spiritual Writing 2013*
"Packing Slip" was reprinted in *The Torah: A Woman's Commentary*, URJ Press, 2008

The Two Yvonnes

Next Door

Robbie Gross is dribbling, then fakes a shot, then takes it,
the metronome of his solo practice an accompaniment
so persistently tapping its foot in my days that, 4 a.m.,
forty years later, hearing a basketball *tock*
on the sidewalk below my window, I am returned
to my first room, separated by a mulberry tree
and hedges from where Robbie Gross is dribbling, then
fakes a shot, then takes it, the metronome so persistently
tapping its foot in my days that I knew we were keeping time
but what song was it during games with our older brothers
and after they left, shooting by himself, like the tree
alone falling, morning and long afternoon, through my
books, through all my ages—what song? I broke
the court's code and deciphered the slow dribble's: *I'll.*
Wait. while the shooter sized up the competition or
focused his solitary mind, and then the bomb-fuse *ticktickticktick*
while he feinted right, moved left, setting up the shot
and the listener (not trying to listen) and then the blank
space of the arcing quiet as he shoots. That silence
is also like the space between the reader and the page,
the little nation between the writer's words and our
particular way of receiving them, or the blank station
we fill in between ourselves and passing strangers,
or between ourselves and people we presume to know,
but most achingly in the ones we try to know.
Then came my guess whether the shot went in, hit the rim or
bounced off the garage, because I had the misfortune
of growing up next-door friends with the pudgy Rob Gross
who became the most handsome Robbie, growing taut

and sly for having played from the outside line for so long
and by his last June when the beautiful Margie Harmelin
rode over from her neighborhood and lay her bicycle
on its side before they both went indoors, by then
he only caught my eye with reticence, a muffled kindness
passing to me from under his shaggy bangs,
nearly embarrassed for me, as I now understand it,
because he was bluff enough to know what he had become
to any young woman, and what I was becoming in my
blank space, my window, like this one from which I just
heard Robbie Gross take a shot, from which I just
dreamed hearing the song the world called "Don't. Wait."

Promised Town

You hoped your string of tickets
would last all day, or someone's parent,
protectively wandering the Fund Fair,
would buy you more because
as it worked out, they cared for you.
Those were the two hopes.
The land behind high school had never
been bigger, or more friendly.
Your older brother's friend,
working the Treasure Chest booth,
set you up behind the mound
of keys and schooled you
in how to fish for luck. But
the main attraction was the fair
itself, that it fit, nearly uniquely,
the illustrations set before us
in books and movies, of our lives,
and now, on one blessed
let-it-last Saturday afternoon
we could try winning, wandering
to a score of circus music
as real kids. Who can explain
why our good fortune—
handmade by our parents
and carted piece by piece into
our days—why it retained
a fated weightlessness, and why
our childhoods maintained
a haunted feeling of the inauthentic,

as if we orbited outside
the promised town, outside
its Main Street, and with no relation
to the promised girl skating
on the Town Grove's frozen pond,
her magenta scarf a gift ribbon
below her very yellow blonde flip,
which was why the teacher titled
the mural "Our Winter"—
so we might be her, although
we had never seen her. But the seasons
had moved on. We were very
warm at the fair, and our favorite
booth, the one that always settled
the question once and for all,
was where we now stood.
Its metal tub looked like a tire
cut in half, and hummed with power.
We watched an upperclassman
move a paper cone around the entire
hollow, twirling it as he went,
again and again like the earth
twirling in rotation while it circled
the sun in massively speeded-
up years, and the invisible wisps
became during some moment
we could never quite pinpoint
pink and real cotton candy
that disappeared inside the little
cosmos of our selves within
a blink, as it had spun to life,
as time would spin and sink,
and luck appear, and disappear.

House Phone

The house I grew up in was ringing,
the whole house a telephone,
and I could pick up any part like a receiver.
The small, high window in my bedroom
was speaking, so was the staircase
curve and grade, all were speaking;
the house itself was a message
uttered in footfalls while I walked
from hallways to rooms,
and it was a language from my own
old country, its seasons passing
over the little window like the scroll
of a small story, the way the sky
is a window and the constellations
a story in hieroglyphs, and the message
of the unclimbable pine and inedible
pear trees collaborated with wind
and the gill-like shutters on sound,
and the curtains advised sun
about shade, how it idled
like teenagers against walls in rooms
we weren't in, and the couch spoke
about snow's reflection in its arms
like a mischievous bride early
mornings—everything within our
property lines had decided to orate
the history of some particular inhabitants
who were us, and for the purpose
of those moments each bookshelf

held a charge in our hearts, as did
the seat which unfolded near the stove
like a ticket taker's in a booth
and the handily referenced Farmer's
Almanac hanging on a string, all
the obliging drawer handles,
the shallow cabinets for cans,
the entrance hall's beaded mirror—
a souvenir from a market in a town
that once was the only place in the world
to buy it, and now the mirror
had become a souvenir of all our
coming-and-going glances
and might be considered a document
of life in quicksilver, how modern
and filled with modern knowledge
we feel until the next day
seeing yesterday's self and things
upon returning, and leaving. Finally
I opened the door to the basement
and found the wall-mounted
pencil sharpener whose handle I turned
like an old phone's, then wrote
a request to my future on lined paper
that I folded, with a Dickinson poem,
behind a knot in the paneling.

Anthology

My first city came in hard cover, off a shelf,
a metropolis where the skyline was founded
in each poem's title, and skyscrapers
stretched to the bottom margin. When I
turned the page I turned the corner,
because what is the difference between
blank space and the air of your town?
Early on I found a poem as squat and devilish
as a pub. Another, broad as boulevards,
conveyed expansive thoughts with girth enough
for medians and benches. A horse
and carriage clopped along; I liked the noise
and rode it twice. Bundling through alleys
of milk bottles and motorcycles, I stopped
before a storefront that tipped the future—just now
I understand this—toward me, shimmering,
beyond my purchase. Wiser customers
bought it, and broke it in along the avenues.
For our sake, here, I'll say that that one book
held all a city and that that one day was like my life.
Noon, I read a poem that spoke like
a no-nonsense bra-fitter, and then another
like a candidate for mayor. Some peddled
used wares with a plea and a jig, and others
trafficked in rough trade through smooth lyric.
My favorites showed themselves plainly,
invitingly, like an open-air plaza
where one might rest at a table and write,
and some sang down and up like musical fountains

such a plaza might offer, or the modern museum—
in fact the volume was lousy with private collections!
Public squares were packed with pillow talk
and I liked that fluff, wanted to hear it all,
and respond in kind, as to the traveling voices
in the Oyster Bar's arcade and the curved
bench at the Botanic Gardens where no secret
can be said too softly to hear, or ever enough.
As for the inhospitably inaudible, the cold-
slab districts contrived from unappealing materials,
I navigated these as well, because a city
must make room for everything and think
of everyone, even those who prefer to
feel excluded. Peckish by three, I found
a hole-in-the-wall where lunch saved the day,
and drowsy from bread and meat, I lazed by
magazine stands, triangular parks and embassy
steps. Dusk moved in, and if you are born
disenfranchised, you feel it again, then,
wondering, dizzily, where you will live.
I turned onto a block of lamplit brownstones
that looked comfortably related—
the stretched family sharing large porticos
like big eyebrows—and a frame house
whose ill symmetry seemed fresh
from the country. It began to snow
paper. I retraced my beat and got lucky:
I found the apartment where a handsome
but unshaven face looked out at me and shouted
from the top floor window, *Buzzer's broken!*
then threw his keys down to my feet.

What We Read Then

Before Young Adult there was Mason Williams' *Reading Matter*
with that fabulous chapter called "Salad Days" which
I know would make me laugh again, and that one
little poem where he says he envies the pool his girlfriend
dives into because it touches her so completely—oh if
we could ever imagine being thought of that way—
and Peter Beagle's *Last Unicorn*; there was *Seven Arrows*
by Hyemeyohsts Storm, declared later by scholars to be
a hoax, and the book in handwriting (not for children)
called *Living on the Earth* by Alicia Bay Laurel, who had
changed her name and here explained everything
about communal living, peasant blouse patterns and how to
rid yourself of crabs if I remember correctly; when short
a utopia, we dug into Plath, and there was Salinger, of course,
who had set up the speakers for the other guys to use
then ran around backstage in black when the lights
were out so we could never see him again, and we read
every single book by Hermann Hesse—we would have read
the outtakes if he had them; we nodded yes to *Be Here Now*,
we hid with *Coffee, Tea or Me,* which we honestly believed
was written by two stewardesses (we ourselves might be)
instead of by a male hack, dreaming, and then Anaïs Nin—
because whatever sex was, we were in, especially if it
sounded like "Angel in the Morning" which we had reason
to believe it did; we built toward Vonnegut, for forgotten reasons
we liked Brautigan; we lived through *Separate Peace*
and *Lord of the Flies,* the far worst being *A Bell for Adano,*
whose title alone still makes me feel like cinder blocks
are tied around my brain, and all the while we never thought

a sentence wasn't true or an author wasn't who the cover
said she was, even *Go Ask Alice* whose anonymous author
went on to write many other anonymous fake diaries
each about a teen who suicided from one wrongheaded
decision or other (as some of these real authors did).
But by the time the truth snaked through the interference
the books sat solidly in our minds like cross-legged girls
in a circle around a campfire, maintaining
an innocence the way the innocent who are brought to court
remain linked to the charges of which they were cleared.
Then, my last night at camp, asleep in my bunk,
I was slipped a copy of *Zen Flesh, Zen Bones* with its
yellow cover. Even now, when daily identity falls dark
I still seek out its traveling monks and enigmatic masters,
and when I think of how publishers lied to us then,
I have to wonder if Americans who believed the corrupt
administrations of the 21st century's chilling turn
are more or less like we were as young adults
in the public library, peering sideways at bindings
with the faith that deer in a leafless winter keep for bark.

The First, Youngest Men

Were not artful enough by half, but we got over
On their sweat, summer's condiment, and magnificent
Proximity, as if actors had stepped offstage
To climb in our laps. Sometimes they were so lanky
Their corduroys could not shape to their hips
And hollows, and then we were warmed by the rays
Their pelvic bones sent over the horizon of their belts,
And sometimes their heft eclipsed a tender manner
So surprising we did not know what would come next
And we were frightened. We loved their long hair,
Their brotherhood with guitars and drums, and something
The ages should not overlook is that we were magnetized
By peacefulness, and by people who desired it. Memory
Adopted those t-shirts, left hanging on a branch
By the lake, that had enjoyed the confidence of their collar
Bones and chests; whichever sweater their mothers
Had lifted from dresser to trunk we took to heart its pattern
And feel against our chin; whatever posture they took
In opposition or even admiration for authority impressed
On us the dash of their autonomy, and where they
Touched us we went phosphorescent, like the lake's skin
Sparking as a diver breaks it, for breath. The tang of pine
Boughs and cold offset, as if arranged, their warm hands
And neck, and there was the weight—that defining
Body-long entrance to our space—while the constellations
Floated, years before they pressed down on our men
With the spite of the abandoned, a handful at a time.

Seven, Seven, Seventy-Seven

We held a party that night, for the sheer luck of it
landing in our time and never to happen again
until maybe eleven, eleven, eleven, although the city
was hurting from a crop of dope-driven thieves
who broke in a second time to get the ice cube trays,
and from Son of Sam (we were unused to worrying
about *one* person), all under broiling temperatures.
My return each evening from apprenticeships
at the travel writer's apartment or the magazine office
became a riddle born from domineering mercury:
watch straps, sandals, sleeves—how to live
with them? I prized a dress so thin it agreed not to
touch the body, and dinner could not be anything
that had been heated, ever, so, out of the subway
to my sublet on Duke Ellington Boulevard, dreaming
of a cold shower, I stopped into the Japanese grocery
for a few slices of sashimi. Thank goodness I was living
with someone else's belongings because in July
I accuse objects of generating heat and tend to toss
dear tokens of my own past. Even so, that summer
defined a divide and introduction. The travel writer's
composer-friend had made bundles on an airline jingle
but I also heard a canon he wrote for forty cellos—
a school of dolphins, rising and diving—and the magazine office
was filled with the great feminists of the second wave,
the central hallway posting news clippings of legal
victories or blockades of what we now accept
as basic civil rights. Time leaves behind the obvious
as plain as day, like seashells when the tide goes out.

You might have had such a summer, when your boyfriend
drives all night from Detroit and the next day
you lie on the park lawn, chatting with him, waiting
in line for free tickets to Shakespeare. It was that kind.
A week after the party, taking out the dinner garbage,
I let slam the heavy door to the service hall;
the lights went out, the reggae cut off, the refrigerator
shushed. "Lights! Lights!" shouted the residents
on the south side of the street (who never got sunlight
to begin with), torso-out of their windows, holding candles
to a city gone powerless. We took the transistor with us.
The looting had begun on Broadway; men carried
baseball bats, which anyone could tell you is the wrong
object in front of a jewelry store. The audio shop
went next—"Riot Sale Inside!" written on cardboard
in the storefront—and subway riders streamed up
as if from anthills. I think stars were seen above the city
before the lights came back. By mid-August, Son
of Sam was caught by then-obvious clues. One morning
as it was all coming to a close, my boyfriend and I
were outside, saying goodbye. He leaned against
a building, a duffle bag of laundry by his feet and Jimmy
Cliff shades pushed up on his head. "Sonny,
are you going into the navy?" asked the old woman
in a nightgown, from her ground-floor window,
her German shepherd in attendance. But our battles
only took the form of seasonal discomfort, class-
action lawsuits, daily separations. The toes feel it
first when autumn's tide rolls in, and with late
August's pair of socks I remember our rising good
fortune, how it slicked the soles of our feet
like sweat and left us these shells when it ebbed.

The Voice of Peace

It was just the radio, me, and ten turkey coops
in need of shoveling. Hot. Very. But—
and this will give you an idea about that summer
as a whole—a relief. In fact, I'd lobbied
for the freedom of the coops, anything
to get me out of the kibbutz' kitchen
with all those trauma victims pecking at me no
matter how I peeled a carrot or cleaned a floor.
It seems I'd fallen through some confusing crack
in Israel, or my brain itself became partitioned
and now I only remember the residents
thwacking me on the bus queue in Tel Aviv,
elbowing me at the grocery, and when preparing food
they were not at their best, but I had signed on
for socialism and the freedom to play
a Robert Palmer album in the basement room
allotted for the volunteers at night
where we had more tea, more biscuits,
and hallelujah, shesh besh with the other volunteers,
still vivid wanderers through the orchard rows
of memory. And though it was not a good
match, my person and that particular kibbutz,
I did find love and traveled on to Greece,
and while attempting my part in the great experiment,
attempting to dovetail my history with a homeland,
I remember fondly The Voice of Peace
coming from a corner of the coop, off and on
through the static and translation, my privacy
intact, my job straightforward and finite,
my picture of the boat out there off all
our shores, a friend to anyone who listened.

Houston in the Early Eighties

before iced coffee came to town, a sump from which I've fished
many a memory of regret and loneliness and whose misery
I now understand came less from my pocked nature than from
the choke hold of blue laws, and from my broken-willed Eeyore
of a used car which liked to stop stubbornly in Sealy, halfway to
Hill Country and always one day after the insurance ran out,
and from the paucity of public space so that we drove (locally)
from shopping strip to balding park, once to a leech-infested pond;
and owing also to the blinding afternoons that made invisible,
to the unpracticed eye, micro-lands of existing urban hip, or just a bench
on which to read the paper, the scarce sense from city planners
that those residents without garden-crusted homes held their own set
of municipal needs which might take the form of some kind of . . .
beauty; together with the impossibility of finding deep
shade or hearing wind flash through trees, the abundance of short
rainstorms or hurricanes, both of which, equally, caused water to boil
out of the sewers and flood the car (which wouldn't, then, even be
starting out to break down in Sealy without borrowing again
to fix it); and the living rooms' glass sliders opening without apology
onto the apartments' walkway and courtyard, motel-style,
furthering the shallow sense of experience; and all this witnessed
by two small universities whose meek students made no protest
that their fourth-largest city in the United States—a town sporting more
soft-food cafeterias than all churchgoing people in the world
could possibly attend at once—offered but two art cinemas
and nearly nowhere to wander or peruse, nowhere to make peace
with the simple fact of your twenties. And on such a day as this,
the one I walked through this morning in late June, on such a day
we would have gathered those friends we could draw from their corners,

their condos, their garage apartments humming to beat the cicadas,
and we would meet in one driveway with a particular lock-and-key
of desperation-and-relief I have been lucky enough not to feel since,
a collective village slamming the doors on our town, plugging in
a tape as we took off for Galveston, because if it was going to be endlessly
    flat
it might as well be on a beach, regardless of the soupy knee-high water
or the thwapping mullets jumping out of it, and we might as well be
together on a blanket in the middle of the dessert drinking something
cool enough to slake one of all our many raging, hissing thirsts.

Without Measure

She was stick-thin in pedal pushers
and wasted by the cancer just months
after they found it. All those wasted years
at Weight Watchers, stepping on the scale
before the *tskking* ladies in their folding
chairs who watched the silver rung
lugged further to the right. Queen
of the honeydews, insomniac baker, sister
to the other grandmothers who measured
without scales or spoons because proportions
felt like wool goods they could rub
between their fingers. Wrung out by wifely
servitude, she husbanded her energies
to serve the Jewish unwed mothers,
and the children at a place they called a school,
but was really an asylum. Finding them
chained, alone and filthy, she held them
close, a volunteer floater from a world
of mercy, and soothed them without
measure. At the time of our last story
I had been away six months, though seeing
her I realized I had also been away for
sixty pounds. She served my favorite fish—
the gold-tin of the chub skin garnished
with a parsley sprig. You always were
a bag of sugar in my life, I dreamt I said
as my goodbye, though at her door
I saw she was to end thin as a willow
twig that pities the poor fire into starting.

Stowaway's Ascent

The footsteps were unanimous, an urgent
ovation which I took as the most wrong
moment to show myself. If compassion
struck the hull to pull us down who could
show compassion then to one such as
myself? But eventually the storm moved
on, silence proclaimed the shipmen gone
and I lay on my back in high quiet, as volumes
must feel, hidden and saved and unopened.
Next I felt strangely like Abraham, the pebble
chosen from gravel to have an experience
for everyone, to ascend the abandoned deck
where the masts spoke as if to themselves,
and even the life boats were barely visible,
like disappearing sentences of our past day-
long discussions. I came here to be with him
and I came fourth: first him, his mate, his crew,
then me. Surely you know this moment
when you survey the endlessness and lone
stretch of time? Obsession, they say, stands
in for obfuscation, like a buzzing swarm
of protestors who drown the truth, or try.
And I had lain below obsessing in my berth,
and now, the sky unveiled, I heard nothing,
and there was nothing to argue, deny or confirm
aside from the need to find water, and land
and learn the language of the gulls to whom
I'd thrown all my crumbs before we sailed.

One Key

It seems odd that just one key
lets me in my front door
and into my life every day. New York City
doors used to require a series
of accomplishments: clicks, grinds
and releases from ordered keys, each
performing a specified task reliant
on the one before, like a hand-powered
factory of letting-you-in. Rarely
could you use a friend's keys
without locking yourself out or
staying locked out while snow
flew sideways and table lamps heckled
from their self-satisfied windows.
Apartment keys in the late twentieth century
composed a pattern particular
to their owner's life right then
and being able to puzzle a friend's
skeletal set implied you knew
the person inside out. For college
students, locksmiths were the living
dialectic, and their most impressive
challenge were "police locks"
that began from four feet away, a bar
slanting, like a running dive
from it's brace on the back of the door
to its notch in the floorboards.
Secured behind the whole arrangement
were only records and books

(our other identifying trait)
but the *clank glink* of getting to them
seemed appropriate: like so much
goes on between two people
and even in one person's mind on a given day
many sorts of locks are necessary.
Now I turn one brass key
to the left and the wooden doors
open onto everything about us.

Packing Slip

White, Jewish female, 5' 4½", 112 lbs, brown eyes, brown hair, from hirsute tribes in Poland and Russia, Tay-Sachs positive, HIV negative, anemia prevents selling blood for pocket money when traveling in Greece or other countries, Raynaud's disease causes numbness in digits when cold, often followed by sense of homesickness for some place as yet unnamed; fallen arches from thirty years of running the streets of Roslyn, Manhattan, Houston, Brooklyn, and wherever she woke up; aversion to cilantro, and violent response to tickling; wide scar down belly from amateurish removal of ovarian cyst; slight knife-fight scar on shoulder from lung surgery with side-effect of permanent tenderness in left breast; pregnancies to term: 2; abortions for medical reasons: 2; for non-medical: 1; miscarriage followed by d&c: 3; able to swim a mile without shortness of breath and lift heavy packages in single heave; fine sense of smell although Semitic nose reflects, through complexion, emotional climate, intake of hot drinks, alcohol, spices and chocolate; can sit cross-legged and touch toes (separate times), stalled lifelong at 11 push-ups; legally blind without specs, sensitivity to sunlight has bred the wearing of sunglasses indoors in such places as rude brightness requires; no fear of bats, snakes or spiders, but scurrying rodents evoke generic screech. In general, however, heart seems unafraid: shows buds, rings and other surprising signs of new growth and heartiness for winter months; flowers and fruit collected last spring still out for analysis; lab technicians have reported falling into dream-like faint upon attempt to decode spell and provide explanations. Contents, which may have settled during living, contain live cultures. Inspector #9

A Line from Jimi Hendrix Comes to Mind

in the giraffe house as another one sails
mast first through the wall and the shyest one licks a cloud
from the scenery. It is nineteen degrees outside

so they are in here, a room the size of your parlor but
limned with a far-off horizon
and you notice the tennis-ball lump in their chin trembles

like an aunt's whiskered throat as if waiting for a tea tray
in the painted savannah. It is so private here today,
I lay on the visitors' bench to nap—

and now they step like nurses walking quietly
outside a sick room but my daughter's friend said,
O the smell! Let's go outside!

and there, between the treetops' bare limbs
two days after New Year's
we saw the nests borne up to the blue

and you know how it is, how I am, how the entire zoo
becomes a warehouse for a thief who reaches for the highest
shelf to kiss what she might like to call her own.

Early April

Helpless to the spinning world around me . . .
—*Becki Marcus*

The cyclists can't help seeming self-important
and the daffodils can't help interloping
on the edges of dark gardens; the shaggy birches
can't help tending them in peeling robes
and the purple crocuses can't keep from clashing
with the orange noise of birds; the spring
can't help its interruptions and the morning
can't help its illusion of beginning, again
beginning, and the wanderer can't help
squandering the dimes of her small fortune
or wishing the morning could be the first line
of a drawing her daughter began again; what if
this was our first day, Becki, and the bulb
of the heart humming in frost all those months
came up as you were riding by, the orange
birds requesting your attention and the first light
falling on your dark eyes, knowing it was good?

"This" and "That"

Because I imagine you both as flat-footed plainclothesmen
collaring ideas
like perps for a lineup,
you have something in common with the God
who flies up, also male,
from the sentence I am reading
like an intake of breath,
past the guards at the gates of the mind,
a little ghost to fill the word "God,"
even as I remind myself I have no God
(and if I did, she wouldn't be bearded).

So much of our coloring-in
would turn more *Glinda* than *Eastwood*
if the unassigned were female.
It got to us, all those years of He, His and Him,
all that Fe Fi Fo Fum,
all that rain seeping through the roof's flashing and tar
into the mind's living room
till drip, drop on the page
while we are reading.
From overhead, the slap of footsteps, the men
still fixing the leak.

When My Daughter Got Sick

Her cries impersonated all the world;
The fountain's bubbling speech was just a trick
But still I turned and looked, as she implored,
Or leaned toward muffled noises through the bricks:
Just radio, whose waves might be her wav-
ering, whose pitch might be her quavering,
I turned toward, where, the sirens might be "Save

Me," "Help me," "Mommy, Mommy"—everything
She, too, had said, since sloughing off the world.
She took to bed, and now her voice stays fused
To air like outlines of a bygone girl;
The streets, the lake, the room—just places bruised
Without her form, the way your sheets still hold
Rough echoes of the risen sleeper, cold.

Beauty's Rearrangements

I had been thinking about everything being
relative, especially our considerations
of joy and grief,

which led me to thinking about the universe,
and not finding any other planet like ours
within light-years

and other units of distance—which themselves
have no beginning but tend toward
bunches of billions—

my mind picked up on where it had left off fraying.
Thankfully my god of reconciliation
(New York City)

collects string, sometimes tying it together. One
night, when December wound a black
scarf around the streets

of Williamsburg, Becki and I wandered into
the lit beauty of a yarn shop
open only after six;

shelves lined the walls like mini-bunk beds
and resting skeins filled them
in colored waves

of quiet to bright to dark and back, toward
and away a center that rearranged
itself around our gaze;

we were not prepared for relative perfection,
but we became instructed by it.
The pregnant clerk

held to her chest five shades she herself could not
resist, and we imagined her knitting
the baby's cap

(because even May will feel cold in this new world)
and Becki's choice, High Rose,
was placed on the swift—

a rack like an upside-down umbrella skeleton
which expanded like the proverbial
husband's patiently

raised palms to hold it—and then was threaded
onto the ball-winder which got turned
fishing reel-style,

rotating the swift until the planet of red
was done, and came off neatly.
And, here, I racked

my brain for up and down, where might the universe
hold us in regard, because sometimes
our joyous combinations

turn renegade, like the runaway Pleiades, or our
idyllic summers play in other hemispheres
as grievously cold,

but when the yarn was handed over still charged
with transformation and no strand was
left to fall alone

I saw my eight-year-old delighted by the task
of beauty's rearrangements, and let my
sorrows spin to gold.

What *For* Is For

A portal with two guards
each turned to their left
they thought they heard
something coming
the common sparrow
trespassing, giant-like
in the papery leaves

and their job was to
look out for you, to hold
a place as steady as
a plumb line
while the boat swashed
in a massive current
in a common occurrence

come on
the tall and short one
both shout come through
our door and bring your
family we can't guarantee
your safety if you stay on
your side of the page

Before

The blueberries outnumbered the leaves around the lake, full
blown like balloons tied off at the stem. You could trip them
a handful at a time from the stems, but even so it required much
repositioning of the canoe, and wading, and many landings
to collect enough for a pie, and because we had pancakes,
muffins and sauces, I hoped my girls might feel surrounded
by more of something wonderful than they could use. As you
might expect we sang; we jumped off islands the girls had
named the year before; we smoothed our towels on pine beds
and moss, or sometimes on the jagged rocks that still
gave off perfume from within their vaults; we read from a treasury
about birds, or the poems of the cockroach and his feline friend
who had fallen from her incarnation as Queen Cleopatra
and now wandered the alleys like a diminished Elizabeth Taylor.
One day, looking up, as if there shone the face of whatever god
might change it all, I said, Let's get back home before the rain,
and we paddled to the beat of the wind, as the first fat drop
fell, our bow touched the dock, and that night I turned the little
block of wood sideways against the screen door frame in
case a bear less sated than ourselves called on us in our sleep.

Cosmic Page

Folded in half, the long paper documenting
the history of the self was like a page of Talmud,
chronology woven with commentary, calling
and responding between hope and memory
and invention. We had advanced to those passages
below the crease, and we looked up over
its horizon to the sky at top where floated
our early ideas of what might happen,
what we imagined life might be. Eventually,
as we read and studied, night rolled in around
the text of our earlier selves, which glimmered
through black in constellations without pattern,
as though a seamstress had brandished her
tracing wheel without discrimination, or
conversely, with the determination to map
which thoughts went where and without reason
where next. Each dot became a footprint
in the opposite of snow, spelling out scrambled
paths to danger or doorways. We were just people,
thinking about life. And, as is traditional
with Talmud, we studied in pairs. Lying on our backs,
when our eyes adjusted we talked to each other
as though we had discerned the natural
circuitry behind all the years' yes's and no's,
and we followed the looping, lasso-tying
course of events with hypnotic interest as you
follow the zag-zig of bats in the rafters, like a vole
follows the unseen flight of the raptors
and the log considers the progression of flame.

A Poem for S.

Because you used to leaf through the dictionary,
Casually, as someone might in a barber shop, and
Devotedly, as someone might in a sanctuary,
Each letter would still have your attention if not
For the responsibilities life has tightly fit, like
Gears around the cog of you, like so many petals
Hinged on a daisy. That's why I'll just use your
Initial. Do you know that in one treasured story, a
Jewish ancestor, horseback in the woods at Yom
Kippur, and stranded without a prayer book,
Looked into the darkness and realized he had
Merely to name the alphabet to ask forgiveness—
No congregation of figures needed, he could speak
One letter at a time because all of creation
Proceeded from those. He fed his horse, and then
Quietly, because it was from his heart, he
Recited them slowly, from *aleph* to *tav*. Within those
Sounds, all others were born, all manner of
Trials, actions, emotions, everything needed to
Understand who he was, had been, how flaws
Venerate the human being, how aspirations return
Without spite. Now for you, may your wife's
X ray return with good news, may we raise our
Zarfs to both your names in the Great Book of Life.

Little White Truck

Because the white truck traveling the span of the Williamsburg Bridge
could be the white fastener traveling the top of a ziplock bag,
the East River and tugs might be contained without spilling
in today's October light, along with this new spray of trees and
picnic tables which appeared when the industrial tide of Williamsburg
went out. If these could be contained, then likewise the two cyclists,
now dismounted and steadying their bikes as they kiss, and surely
it could hold the music they heard last night eddying again
around their thoughts, and the memory of their first idea of the future
loosed when he held her in a doorway lit by cobwebs of spring rain.

Sonnets for the Autobiographical Urban Dweller

This little room fills up with light. It's big
when you consider all the ways to re-
configure books, or how the walls bow, rigged
to hold whole lives, which, often, neighbors see
and hear. The urge to frame one's tale takes hold,
then, mirrored, gives you pause. This window's wide,
but honesty as policy? Truth told:
to share shared stories we both show and hide,
or coat our private parts of speech, because
regardless of our tender subjects we
tilt, bare, toward sunlit panes, parlaying flaws
to blushed, polite applause. It's our *esprit*.
Dark days I tend the window box—looks good—
then pull the shades down on the neighborhood.

Baldo's

Your whole life you vow you won't do it again
but some synapse glitch makes it impossible
to remember, and again you walked into a pizza parlor
chosen from an on-line list about a neighborhood
you are visiting for reasons other than dinner,
and the toupee-heavy owner, sadder than
a hound, looks out resignedly at his floor of
empty tables; the heat is off, the hanging
electric menu looks repaired with band
aids, even the touted brick oven looks cool
to the touch, but instead of walking out—because
a restaurant is not supposed to make you wary
or troubled— you accept the notion that the rip
tide of your decision making has swept you
to this place from which it would be dangerous
to turn back, and when I describe the scene
to Miriam she relates her own jaw-setting
response to such moments: "We had better
make the best of it," as though we chose a life
boat with limited supplies, as though our decisions
are so powerful they send a contract up ahead
to the strange neighborhood, and our unfamiliarity
with what else might be around keeps us from
leaving Baldo's and peering across the street
where beckons a sparkling—golden, nearly—
anything, anything else, any other life than ours.

Perfume's Journey

The evening submerged the car in darkness
as though it had been driving down into the earth
instead of to the mountain's top. As we funneled
from expressway, through towns, to dirt lane,
the night immersed the two girls sleeping
in the back seat, their lighted heads just above water,
their last argument dissolved between them.
Our halting conversation was drawn from depths
deliberately, cautiously, cold well water. Throughout,
our tone was gracious, as one might tear off
portions of baguette while thinking it a ticket
to the future. But neither of us felt nourished,
and as the day stripped away—gone behind us
lights, signs, phones, motors, houses, even rain—
I had to wonder where we were going
and how the same roads could bring us to such
different places at hungry times. Almost there,
we were stopped by orange traffic cones
and flashing lights; emergency tree surgeons
had opened shop by unfolding one large yellow
truck. Its growling generator trained klieg lights
on four trees crisscrossed against the power lines;
the cherry-picker basket, stories high, buoyed
one man into the limbs to unknot branches
with a giant crochet hook tipped with buzzing blade
while his grounded partner with compact chain saw
undid limbs from trunks and then trunks from
themselves into sudden logs. So speeded was
the transformation, we should have been prepared

for the gale of sprung perfume outside the car,
but we hadn't considered skin—how many forces
have one—the bare containment of each other's,
power, and our first knowledge of it. By the time
the lifted man levered the basket to its cradle,
stepped down and chose another chain saw,
the girls had emerged and spread a blanket to sit
and watch. Within moments the asphalt lost
its power to the feather bedding of chips and leaves,
and moments after that an entire passage of woods—
history, inhabitants, song—was cleared away.
By now, a few cars' headlights stared from
either side of the truck, like the band of cows
who the lovers, rising damp with evening dew
from a field of thyme and clover, once found
gathered in a ring around them. We drove the last
three miles up the mountain and when we got out
the perfume had followed us up from its trees,
but when we woke the next morning it was gone.

Little "the" Rules the World

One-third of all living things, the beetles.
All the laws, of mathematics, averages
and gravity. The truth; the variations. The
semi-colon. The adaptations. The Chameleon
constellation. The Polynesian wayfarers,
12,000 years ago, reading its directions.
The sails made of pandan leaves. The bee's
waggle dance, inside the hive, conveying
the exact location of the maraschino
cherry processing plant five miles away.
The resulting red honey. The straight
pin through the moth's diversion. You say,
I remember the moment you. Or, the
last straw. The ant colony under the stone
door of the locked castle. Your neck, the
drop of rain that found it. The ongoingness,
evidently complex, of sheer stupidity:
the adaptations. The machete, the box
cutter. The raped. The morning they wake
up to, regardless. The Indefatigable
Galápagos Mouse, extinct. The country
mice. Their log cabin in the medicine
cabinet of the log cabin: Q-tips lashed
with floss, the roof of cotton. The map,
and the "Ode to the Lemon." The latent
energy of transformation, the steam
whistle. The country following fear and greed,
ongoingly. The pregnant girl. The fact
of the end at the helm: the lead bird of the
v, who knows where the flight is headed.

Gardens, Passover

The first seventy-degree April day takes you around the waist
and because you are suddenly too warm in your sweater
not only do you pull it off with annoyance, but you never
want to see it again, because in those seconds it conveys your lifelong
lack of vision, your foolish decisions, and you actually feel
sheepish, as though conservative weather predictions
cast an affront against the whole earth turning, a riff on
the Day of Atonement's notion of everyone taking a twist
for the better all at once, so that the entire body of people
has a chance against the worse parts of our nature, à la
a massive march on a spiritual Washington, the capital
of human governance, or an entire population putting their back
to the cosmic wheel to guide the leaning soul aright. But
this season's holiday has more to do with the system of the locks
on the Mississippi, the footsteps painted on the dance room floor,
the recognition that getting from the here of slavery

to the there of making foolish decisions on our own
requires you say this first, do this second, eat this third,
sing that fourth, read this fifth, up to fifteen, or forty years
whenever your progress sets you down in the right place
which might be today in the Brooklyn Botanic Gardens
where orange tulip petals glow like flashlight hoods
and the magnolia's candelabra lifts a thousand ivory votives
which light the sky to a very, very blue, while the six-week
processional of cherry blossoms incites a pilgrimage
to these transient studios—some trees producing white blooms
in downy, cupped fists, and others in dangling pink fingerprints
the breeze touches to your bare arms when you peel off your
sweater, an act which may raise your standards and soften your heart
to your own mistakes, instructions given by the earth's angle
on the whole orbit, the first right thing to do as a free person.

Streaming Nancy

When the subway doors opened skunk
wafted over the platform, and the confluence
—14th Street: where it all comes together!—
brought on dualities, the dual nature
of dualities, like quatrains made of two
rhyming couplets I would soon read
on the train, and how my friend Nancy
Ralph (even her name going in opposite
directions) talking to me in the rain—well
half in the rain, one of us seemed to be
in the rain at all times beneath the triangular
awning of Three Lives & Co.—how Nancy
looked like a motorcycle moll and *sage
femme* all at once, and that's pretty true
for the experience of talking to her which,
if I could graph our conversations, would be
something like *Dive! Dive!* because
we're instantly deep, deep in conversation
and the currents of philosophy (Nancy)
are swirling in a current of subject matter
(that'll be me) and in this case we were talking
about the nature of love and after I said
it resembles being caught in a huge yearning machine
she said, "I'm glad to hear you say that
because I've never found it to be a *good* feeling—
it *doesn't* feel good" and I remembered
first knowing Nancy and being at a wedding
where she wore a suit approximating bright
green sod, because she came from Oklahoma

and read *Women's Wear Daily* for her first
whole year in Manhattan and that's why her
magenta bra strap taught so much, and how
the day I came home from the hospital,
a big strange mammal, she brought brand-new
Bella a roll of yellow, starry tulle as a gift,
and how, months later, we dressed the baby up
as a pirate, a red bandanna knotted over the top
of her baldy head, and strolled her around
the neighborhood, and one good thing
about middle age is how many such experiences
you can have with one person who still
meets you in the rain at a book party
even with all she's accomplished in her own
life which I would have to list in a list
poem in *Ripley's Believe It or Not*
including the little-clay-devils-in-a-bottle
project, the poetry-vending-machine
and *The New York Food Museum* entire,
and by the time she waves goodbye, back
to her ex-weaving factory apartment
on the Lower East Side, now Chinatown,
I'm primed to enjoy the after-party itself,
and hard not to since the smashed
poet said to me, who maybe she thought
was someone I might know, like Nancy, "You
should *congratulate* yourself on your very
existence on this earth!" to which I replied
with an astonished *are-you-okay*-look,
and everyone had written their addresses
on one napkin that was going to be transcribed
to one person's computer and e-mailed,
but you know, it was raining pretty hard
and that was not a Sharpie we wrote with
and I was thinking about marriage, that duality,

how you create an island in the middle
of two streaming disappointments (here,
Jed may disagree, disappointed; I'd be
disappointed if he didn't) just sitting together
surveying the meandering, frothing
happinesses caused by your rock and stones
of friends and kids, and as I walked home
the wet leaves on the shiny night sidewalk
looked like pennies in a fountain and I thought
that was pretty funny since I felt so hugely
unlucky (regardless of the local, national
and international reasons I had no earthly right
to) until seeing Nancy, until waving goodbye

The Use of Metaphor

Last night's rain plastered twigs and acorns, Jackson Pollack–style,
atop the porch table in such balance that the weathered lumber
became a canvas I was loathe to revise. We can talk like this all day:
how frogs jump on rusty bed springs at six a.m. and birdsong
lowers like a chandelier; bandit clouds blindfold the sun,
and in their getaway they yank smoke off the water like a loot bag,
but their stolen coins spill onto the lake and glint in new light.
In what terms shall I speak of my daughter pitted against an illness
that would strip her true nature of its wildflowers and moss,
leaving her as if on a bed of rock, unforgiving below a lone leaf
which shudders and surrenders beneath November's interrogation?

God

We lived here long enough to go through all the cycles
of belief and rejection of belief until we arrived
at the deal-making portion of our story, especially
the parents making a deal for the health of their children,
though we had nothing of comparable equivalence
to barter, and when the deals fell through
there was no court of law. It was like walking through
a doorway, using all our strength, intuitively, against
a thread that broke the moment it was recognized
by your palm. Just cobwebs. Bella once said
she thought God was a deer because as soon as you see it,
it's gone. The longer this goes on the more the air
seems filled with strings attached to a history
now as invisible as the deer behind the bushes which
have closed up as if never disturbed, part of the plan.

The Gold Standard

You are mine, every day's penny
candy, slipped disk of the sun's
currency, worthy unit beyond
whether or not, beyond inclemency,
the brick, the vein, the panned
for fancy in daily brooks, the ring
of truth, the measure of every
autumn's filigree and every other
man or treasury, the karat, the stick,
the stay, the filling, the stars atop
a willful diary, each page's edge
in our hardbound book, spending, still
spending, without worry of penury.

Marriage Made in Brooklyn

Ours was a marriage made in Brooklyn. There was too much
bickering for it to be in heaven. Bicker, bicker, bicker.
Who would have predicted it? But Brooklyn's a very fine place
and bickering rules the day even here. It starts early,
with the squirrels squealing on the phone wires
because there's not that much backyard per square squirrel,
and they get nervous about how much there is to eat.
There are the birds, with their own racket, a twig at stake.
Come seven-ten, there are the children being led to the school,
and some of them, you can tell, would prefer a morning
in bed with cartoons and cereal galore, their afternoon,
if it ever came, over a hill with a playground in it.
But they don't really think ahead because that is the work
for people like us who bicker about what is up ahead.
The morning moves into third gear, and the bus bickers
in a heave-ho sigh with the cars, the cyclists mutter
because doors of parked cars swing out at them like pinball flippers,
and by mid-day the planes argue over your conversation
with your neighbor who is peeved at neighbor-to-the-left.
The drivers have to honk to keep the day going because
at two o'clock, give or take, the day can very easily stop.
At that point no one understands why they are doing
what they are doing, or why they should possibly interrupt it
for anything else. Everyone has to nudge the afternoon,
we all make our contributions, and then, the kids are out of school!
Hardly had they gone in! They come out like molecules
that have been holed up in a pill bottle while the whole sky
hammered at the cap. I wouldn't call what they do bickering—
they are pushing and shoving in an attempt to make a universe

out of the sidewalk. Rush hour starts early, ends late.
When my husband comes home it sounds like onions
hitting the hot oil, a spat-upon-arrival born
from two sets of expectations meeting in the middle
like cymbals in the four seconds it takes to say,
Why didn't you kiss me hello? But it's a city of bridges.
Whichever island we travel to we are generally glad.
We live on a busy thoroughfare, for which we have great sympathy
and respect. In bed we lie beneath a canopy of sound
from the comings and goings. In summer, friends chat to each other
and their words pepper our dreams. Sometimes they curse
upon finding they are no longer friends. Taxis whisper in the rain,
but at that point there's no place we would like to be conveyed.
Spring breeze and the white shutters have known
each other forever, they go way back, and all this happens to us
without agreement or disagreement. In autumn the chaotic
frisson of brushing leaves gives the impression of cheerleaders
with pom-poms, urging on the winter. Which reminds me
of the question posed by the Zen master. Does the wind
disturb the trees? The answer shall be the rest of your life.

Gratitude's Anniversary

One August afternoon, decades before,
when the company of my peers felt like
rows of folding chairs I had to walk between,
I took off my fringed moccasins, climbed
over the corral's split-post fence, and made
my way through Mt. Tremper's evergreens
to the stream below, whose song I followed
like the thread of conversation. Hurray
for pine needles, was the message sent up
from the soles, and there was the copse-hidden
brick oven where once we baked a pie from
wild berries. I wasn't allowed in the woods
alone; I was eleven. When I sat with my feet
in the water, just sat, ho, hum, a langoustine
darted out from a rock, like laughter, and I knew
I had come to a place of thrill and peacefulness,
heaven on earth. That day is related to this one.

What to Expect

I woke in pools of milk, like Alice fared
in pools of tears, the morning you were three
days old. I'd read a lot, I'd been prepared,
—if toothpicks can prepare themselves for trees—
but nowhere had I read that mothers' breasts
(when pressed in face-down sleep, and, interrup-
ted by the baby's cries) released, as crests
of waves leave whiteness on the shore, the cups

and cups that overflowed. Your eighteenth year,
I wake, face up, in cold and shocking pools,
this time, of sweat. I'd read about the fear-
some heat that flares inside, and all the schools
of thought that hold no cure. Who could prepare
for how you'd come, then go, a forest cleared?

My Hands in Winter

Their backs, when flat, are like the ice of lakes
on which the wind has skated all these years
recording in a trawling script their work
in bare reconnaissance: to fish for keys
in blowing snow, or hotly sunk, to test
the bath and wash a life of pots. Within
the mesh of figure 8's now scrawled around
our joints are also etched initials of
the loves we lifted, then set down, held close
and when our time ran out, let go. Time flowed
like water through our hands and so the words,
hello, goodbye, are dyed below their ice
like watermarks a sheet of paper names
when raised, as waving hands are, to the light.

Firefly

Lightning it wasn't and camera flash
it couldn't be, not in this high story or late hour
of life. I kept waking up happy
(or I kept falling asleep) to a mini-lighthouse—
patient, steady—in the rafters' pitch,
whose on-and-off fit all days' end:
the yes and no, our land and sea,
the halves and opposites life pins in pairs.
I blinked, or it did, Tinker Bell
come back with semaphores of positive
and negative, a glimpse of heaven
then of the chasm, the strobe above a ballroom
floor which saw, in fractions, who

we were and who we weren't, when now
you saw us now you didn't. O
magic spark, you something-from-nothing,
before I fell asleep, your miner's cap
excavated headlines in their black
and white from deeper in the checkered world
then left the bad news in the dark,
and though I floated full upon my back
and wished to stay where half-full joy
defined this life, I saw you last
as signals from our other side, white jottings
practiced steadily and patiently,
pressed in a code too soon gone black.

One Block from the Navy Yard

Every now and again fortune turns a corner
and there dally the first dandelion flowers
where the jail was razed, and on the stoops
across the street sit families who moved in
when they could only afford the divvied, shy-
of-true brownstones with a rented view of the five-story
Immigration and Naturalization Services prison,
and now they can see straight through the lot

over the tops of the dandelions already white
and blowing right and left, to a street like theirs,
where residents have also put up window boxes
for the first time, as if both sides had shied
from spiking an inmate's sense of drowning
luck by sending up perennials in the sight line
of her cell but now sit beneath blue, red and gold blooms
with an open gaze, talking before dinner.

The Moment We Can't Stay

Never so inviting as the moment we can't stay,
the cleaned house offers everything we want
though now we turn the key and walk away. Windows frame
the set before it's struck, our next best chance

because the cleaned house offers everything we want
to be: There's an Eden of the swept, and washed cups,
the set before it's struck, our next best chance
before we dressed again, before the stacks of clothes

to-be. There's an Eden of the swept and washed, cups
before we broke them, before we spent the pantry,
before we dressed again, before the stacks of clothes
were all messed up. We smoothed the beds, like promises

before we broke them, before we spent the pantry.
We left a good impression, as if we won't come back—but
that's so messed up. We smoothed the beds, like promises;
we left the centerpiece to blossom without witnesses

We left a good impression, as if we won't come back, but
our better half, a hungry, grateful settler, will return.
We left the centerpiece to blossom without witness in
our Garden of Interior, its knowledge ordered

for our better half—a hungry, grateful settler. We'll return,
though now we turn the key and walk away. Windows frame
our Garden of Interior: its ordered knowledge
never so inviting as the moment we can't stay.

For You Today

Of course there is a jackhammer. And a view, like Hopper,
but happier. Of course there is the newspaper—the daily
herald of our powerlessness. Easy go, easy come: *thwash,*
the next day another, an example of everything that gets done
in the dark. Like the initiative of the crocus from a snow
that was, as it works out, warming them. Or in this case,
the strange October weather warming them. There were the
conclusions we jumped to. To which we jumped. There was
pain, and then there was suffering. Of course there was my
ambition to offer you the world, but one that I have rearranged
to make sense. Here are all the sensations of being alive
at the turn of the twenty-first century, here's how they ring out
against each other, here's how one brings out the sense of
another, here is the sun's yellow falling on the fathomless blue.

No Ideas but in Things

We checked the vents and hidden apertures of the house,
then ran out of ideas of where it might be open to the world.
So we couldn't figure out how the squirrel was getting in.
We each had methods that succeeded in shooing him,
or her, out the door—but none of them lasted. Whether
it was the same squirrel—terrified when in the house, and
persistently so—or various, we couldn't tell because
tipped off by a glance, he zig-zagged from froze-to-vapor,
vanishing, Zorro-like, until signs would tell us he had
revisited the sideboard to dig in the begonia. (Escaping
Newcastle to search for coal.) We plotted his counter-
escape, laying a path of pecans to a window opening
into the yard. A few days would pass, and, believing him
gone, we felt inexplicably better than when we began.
Then, from another room, the amplified skritch of nutmeg
being grated—and, crash. Bracelets off dresser tops, bud
vases, candy dishes, things houses have that the backyard
doesn't. You don't think of squirrels knocking things over,
but inside it was like living with the Ghost and Mrs. Muir.
When we couldn't trust the quiet or prove his absence,
we cast him as that hapless shade: worry. Our own gray
area, scat-trailing proof of feral anxiety. But after a few
cycles of release-and-catch I grew bored with the idea,
with its untamed projections. Since he dashes up walls
(yanked, like a pulley), or seeks treasure in a five-inch pot,
daily, why not adopt him as optimism's traveling rep?
I tried. But the sun comes up, we step toward the stove,
and he shoots out like a cue ball, banks off the kitchen door
—what mayhem is caused by going to make coffee!—

and the day, again, begins with a shriek. We are now in
week three and I accept that, inside, the squirrel is going
to stand for something else. And so is the May rain
and so is the day you took off your coat and the tulips
joined in with the cherry blossoms and the people came out
and the pear tree petals floated down in polka dots
around the tulips, and even around the cars. We name life
in relation to whatever we step out from when we
open the door, and whatever comes back in on its own.

The Two Yvonnes

For help he said I should read the new translation of a Gogol story called
"The Two Yvonnes," but after I wrote down the title
of course I realized he meant "Ivans," which brought me to the two
Two Yvonnes, one male, one female, whatever her story might be
now that both of her exist in ballpoint on a line of notebook paper.
And because, at my age, facts tend to switch out with mere notions
like star actors being swapped out for lesser-paid stand-ins
the same day I got the time wrong for a friend's book party—
and what could be more spazzy than arriving early for a book party?
Not being an important actor I stayed on the scene and talked
to my friend's husband: Paul, I said, I love your painting, *Ezekiel's
Dream*, which I saw on that postcard you sent out; how big is it?
He air-sketched a rectangle, tall as an old school window,
and I said, Oh, I thought it was more wide than tall,
at least from the postcard. Oh no, he said, it's more tall than wide. I
didn't believe him but I wasn't going to argue. How's *your* painting
　　going?
he kindly asked. I don't paint, I said, barely wanting to admit it
since it's so rare to be asked about work. You're too modest!
he said. We had only met a few times so I explained, No really, Paul,
I only write. Go on! he said, imitating me, *I only write*. Ha ha!
and this sort of exchange continued for some volleys, Paul's guffaws
escalating with each of my more earnest denials. Karen, I said,
finding my friend who was needed across the room because some heavy
guests had started arriving, Paul is mistaking me for another friend of
　　yours
and he thinks I'm a really good painter! This is *Jess*, Karen said
into Paul's good ear, a thought which went directly to the voting booth

and pressed the lever. He nodded, remembering, and then Karen said
    to me,
Your hair! It's so much darker! Darker? I asked . . . hmmm, I stalled,
trying not to embarrass anyone, Yes! she said, happy to be her honest self,
Much, much darker! You used to have much lighter hair! Who
was she, I wondered, this sandy-haired painter who doubled for me
in their imaginations—the second Yvonne in the new translation—
and who are you? You who I thought the star of my story?

The following poems carry dedications:

"Anthology":	to Stephen Ackerman
"Baldo's":	to Miriam Ancis
"Cosmic Page":	to Judy Katz, Patricia Moger, and Carolyn Vaughan
"Early April":	to Becki Marcus
"Firefly":	to The Mt. Riga Association
"The First, Youngest Men":	to Michael Shepard
"Gratitude's Anniversary":	to Patricia Rodrique
"House Phone":	to Dan, Gloria, Lowell, and Matt Greenbaum
"Houston in the Early Eighties":	to Vicki Ward
"Little White Truck":	to Jennifer Barber
"No Ideas but in Things":	to Alice Elliott Dark
"Streaming Nancy":	to Nancy Ralph
"Gardens, Passover":	to Jeffrey Harrison
"The Gold Standard"; "Marriage Made in Brooklyn":	to Jed Marcus, and for the life that led to this work.
"The Two Yvonnes":	to Karen Chase, and Paul Graubard, whose painting is really titled *Ezekial and the Wheel*. I got it wrong.
" 'This' and 'That' ":	to Hara Person
"What to Expect":	to Bella Marcus
"Without Measure":	to the memory of Bess Rubin

With thanks to Paul Muldoon
and the editors and designers at Princeton University Press.
And for those friends whose years of instructive and compassionate generosity
in all forms has inspired, improved, and housed these poems:
Susan Biskeborn, Sean Elder, Johnny Fading, Dorothy Field, Ramie Friedman,
Karen Gruebel, Robert Held, David Kaplan, Kathy Kilian, Jamie Kitman,
Lorraine Maddalo, Frances McCue, Charlene Shepard, Jon Siegel,
Regina Stone, David Theis, Livia Thompson, Shelly White,
Lee Winder, Bill Zavatsky, Barbara Ziv,
and Daniel Housberg, may his memory be for a blessing.

An Alternative to Speech, David Lehman

An Apology for Loving the Old Hymns, Jordan Smith

And, Debora Greger

Armenian Papers Poems l954–l984, Harry Mathews

At Lake Scugog: Poems, Troy Jollimore

Before Recollection, Ann Lauterbach

Blessing, Christopher J. Corkery

Boleros, Jay Wright

Carnations: Poems, Anthony Carelli

The Double Witness Poems, 1970–1976, Ben Belitt

A Drink at the Mirage, Michael J. Rosen

The Eternal City Poems, Kathleen Graber

The Expectations of Light, Pattiann Rogers

An Explanation of America, Robert Pinsky

For Louis Pasteur, Edgar Bowers

Grace Period, Gary Miranda

Hybrids of Plants and of Ghosts, Jorie Graham

In the Absence of Horses, Vicki Hearne

The Late Wisconsin Spring, John Koethe

Listeners at the Breathing Place, Gary Miranda

Movable Islands: Poems, Debora Greger

The New World, Frederick Turner

Night Talk and Other Poems, Richard Pevear

The 1002nd Night, Debora Greger

Operation Memory, David Lehman

Pass It On, Rachel Hadas

Poems, Alvin Feinman

The Power to Change Geography, Diana O'Hehir

Reservations: Poems, James Richardson

Returning Your Call: Poems, Leonard Nathan

River Writing: An Eno Journal, James Applewhite

Sadness and Happiness: Poems, Robert Pinsky

Selected Poems, Jay Wright